fences

John Siwicki

www.jsiwicki.com

ISBN 0-9774118-3-4

For Library of Congress Cataloging-in-Publication Data
please contact publisher

Poetic Art Published by:

SLABY PRESS
W25952 State Road 95
Arcadia, WI 54612
U.S.A.

www.jsiwicki.com

Technical, Cover, and Book design by JBS

For information contact:
ifojsiwicki@gmail.com
slabypress@yahoo.com

Poems

Poems

not fantasy

Flying high above the trees

Is the music of life...

It can be seen

As well as heard

Tasted, felt, and eaten

Every sense...

Caresses our body

Our soul...

This is real

On the table

Grasp it before it's gone...

Life is not fantasy!

phantasmagoria

All I hear is the rain pouring down
From the dark, cloudy sky
Similar to a machine's din
On a relentless journey downward
Slapping homeward against the windows
Not with complaint, but enjoyment
Being pummeled, drop after drop

Outside the leaves of the trees and plants
Are spanked by the drops of falling liquid
Gradually the relentless torrent
Sounds different from rain-
An angry thunder, a tempest, a lion's roar
Fierce, angry, savage...

Then the volume transforms itself
As I listen to it collide into the roof
A hammer driving a path
Desiring to go down

Flat on my back, safe in my bed
I lie with my eyes and mind wide open
As my senses absorb the night

The ceiling begins to glow brightly
Twinkling stars from another galaxy
So close yet possible to grasp
Up to the boundless frontier my hands go
Desiring to hold the stars with my fingertips

Slowly dancing through the air
Until they freely surrender
Unable to break free from my arms
Acting as a leash handcuffing my hands
Clutching them close to my body

My digits begin to move independently
Putting on a show, bending back and forth
With this galaxy of stars as a backdrop…

Shapes sprout from the vast world I see
Suddenly they burst forth, alive and graceful
As I view this display, I plunge into a feeling
Of expectation and notions…

Energy from the storm alive in my mind
Thunder, lightning, a tornado…
Spinning through my imagination…
With me as the guide---

Just then in the confusion of the storm
Eyes close, I melt into a dream world
Perhaps I'll remember this night

My heartbeat rocks me into a trance
Eyelids fluttering kinship to the raindrops
As I hear the beads rap and roll
Down the window into an infinite cosmos

I hear violins singing to each other
As I fall through puffy white clouds
My body glistening from rays of sunshine
Reflecting off of my body
The violins change into chirping birds
Hunting for their breakfast

I feel now is my time!
Walls to tear down, chains to break
Fences to cross, one more step
No fear dancing with the stars
Every day I have breath…

I recall being quizzed at an early age
About why I could not sit still
I had no patience or forbearance
But at times captivated for hours

Building objects from wood and plastic
Able to focus as the sun beats down
Relentlessly melting everything in its view
Oblivious to everything and everyone

Feeling the sense to get away
Moving across time in silence…

Going fast, the experience a blur
Almost a dream-like memory
Watching my feet stir
In a slow-motion fashion

Counting the steps I'd taken
Measuring the distance and the time
Observe progress, watching change

Flawless melodies
Singing snapshots of life

Now my journey begins nevertheless
Without any plan or thought
Changing direction sharply on the spur
Striking familiarity, caused by chance
Not knowing the destination

Is a breath of fresh air
All I know is the turning of the earth
Round and round, night and day

Joy - love - desire - passion - comfort – peace

So near yet so distant…

Separated and isolated from me
A pagination of unfolding fences
Fences that harbor vast areas
Where only few are allowed

Harsh, mournful fences that slowly
Crumble and wither with time
Leaving only a blemish, a scar of the past

A lifetime is sometimes needed
To breach the mangled walls of iron

First view horrifies, then shocks the sweet
Seen as protection at first, then barrier
Shielding the powerful from the languid
As roads are traveled, reason is lost…
A new dream takes its place

Invisible fences are now
Blocking progress and change
Perhaps only realized for a moment

Tide coming in and going out
Without a visible bridge
No door, gateway or opening
Struggle for life…
Every second-minute-hour-day-
Year after year...

The fence of time and space
Controls our existence...

A fence made long ago…
This novelty greeted with open arms
Enriching life... weaving a fabric of labor

Eventually my weary mind weakens
Tired from the relentless ticking of time

The fence of time
Has proved to be too mighty
Shall I rest for a few moments?
Fear of not waking spurs me on

All alone in the desert
Walking along the highway
Looking for something
On the other side of the horizon
Where I am is an empty place

No sound, only wind and my footsteps
Withering like an old piece of wood
Soon the mountains are in distant sight
Fences of stone...
That appear impossible to climb!

Clouds in the sky change into faces
My father is one that I recognize

He urges me to follow and go on
The faces move across the sky on the wind

I enter a massive mountain range…

Emphatic, determined, powerful
Triumphant, I rejoice…
At the summit, I'm liberated
I rejoice in victory!
There the stars are again looking down

An outstretched arm, a fingertip away
Imagining what is behind or beyond…

Off I go to the other side…
Washed by the glowing gleam
I fall off into my dream

Gazing in silence up at raindrops of light
Humming songs to keep the pain
Of my journey away

Tall pines that reach to the sky
Close in around me

The steps taken earlier
Now beat along with my heart

Sounds of the night pierce my mind
I cover my eyes

My face and breath feel warm
No longer tired or weary
My muscles stretch and retract
With power and energy
After deep breaths of fresh, cool, sweet air

I'm off to climb the next fence that waits
Soon the weight of my tired eyes
Proves too powerful, I drift and doze…
Memories spring out of my mind!

Flying in a plane filled with soldiers going home
Bright sun, cold crisp air, hard as stone
Tender loving smiles, safe and secure
A rumbling roar, sharp, rough and raw
Slicing from above and beneath
Thunder passing, learning the law…

Holding our breath, falling safely down
Soon we're all safe on the ground
After crossing a perpetual welkin

On a tricycle, the curly-head boy smiles
With melted ice cream on his face
This all on a bright summer day

Fences that block our way are clear
Some made by others to turn us away
Or fences to gaze upon for years
We build them until they are done
Kind words, love's soft touch, and help
From this, no fence will stand

No chain will hold
The energy of the storm will unfold
All things are but a moment away…

One old, three-story brick house
A good-sized yard, a garden filled
Growing flowers, vegetables, happiness
Bordering a tree line
Near a small parcel of woods
Leading down to a small stream
Where children are wading and playing

See the old screen door of the house
My hand reaches out, the door opens
An old rusty spring squeaks as it stretches

I enter a large hallway with many rooms
Old wooden trim...
Wraps windows and doorways

Up the stairway, round and round…
Up to the third floor
Solid, warm, beautiful oak under my feet
A box kite leaning against the wall
Ready for flight, but where's Grandpa?
I want to fly his kite

Stepping over to the window, glance outside
He is in the garden planting seeds and flowers
A dog barks and runs through the backyard
Chasing boys of a childhood language
Carefully through the garden
Into the woods and down the hill
Across the creek
I cannot see but know what's there…

The children have no problem
Crossing this fence of shallow water
Along the bank, the three-mile waterfall
The rusty, ancient, obsolete bridge
Paint peeling and falling to the ground
Blowing away in the wind
Shaking and rattling while being crossed

A good diving point
Into the pond below the falls
But they prove too great
For the young to ford
Fear, not wisdom, tells them to wait
But this will be the last time
For courage is needed to decide one's fate

Many roads are taken, fences are crossed
Rush to judgement, a careless fall
Lessons learned and never forgotten
My old home with the squeaky door
School playground
Big, oak tree across the street

Old three-story house
Filled with a lifetime of memories
Memories, stacks of photos packed away
In the closets are albums
Filled with a world of flavors
Waiting to be opened, taking the curious
Off to a dream world fantasy of life
Places and astounding drama
Angles and timeless images

I am part of this fantasy
Stored away, waiting for the next witness
Called to survey and discover
This extraordinary place of impression
I've seen people grow old
But through the pictures...
I see them, as they were long ago

A delineation of boys and girls
Women and men, brothers and sisters
They all live in this panorama of memories
Available to anyone who opens the door

Sentimental feelings bubble to the surface
I recollect the images frozen in time
Unrecognizable children at first
My sisters and brothers I soon know

Myself, a small child standing in the kitchen
Hands in my pockets and shoes untied
Not knowing how to pose for the camera

Watching my sister dance
To a melody I can't hear
Pictures of people I've never met

European towns and cities
That have long since changed
A journey to my parents' wedding
Being born allows me to see
Where it took place, what they wore

It reminds me of a scene
From an old black and white movie
Classic with character
A world since forgotten

The military father wore his uniform
Full dress, sharp with badges
Medals and rank

Placing a golden ring
On my mother's hand
Making a promise
Taking a vow this day

Standing with her hand in his
Grasp of love, heartfelt stare
Kiss on the lips…
She wore a dark, genteel suit
Spangled white dots tinged with ivory
Shone a starlit night of radiance
All this in one afternoon, one night
Wedding, dance, celebration…
Looking at picture albums
Locked in a trance

Some relatives, a few friends
Uncles and aunts
People I don't recall

Children that will grow
Soldiers new found love
Blue sky above...

Land that is part of me
Country in my hand, my life
Under my fingernails, deep in my skin
In my blood, flowing through my soul

Celebration, candles on the cake
New bicycle, off to the path lined with trees
A hot summer day, a cool soft breeze

Fishing with dad, fishing with friends
Campfire under the stars, dancing fire light
Sounds of the night, water rolling on rocks

Footsteps that become silent
Content, no idea of the time...
Waiting for the next day to shine
Then smiling faces, this day is new

I see a field and my dad on a horse
Wholeness of man and beast, strong allies
Coupled in a marvelous partnership
Until one is no more…

Heads held high, ready to ride
Over the tall grass, they gallop in stride

A glance at me
Face of wisdom, hair of gray
Down to my hand with an iron grip
He pulls me over the saddle
My arms wrap around him tightly
I smell his life…

To the horizon we gallop
Floating on the breeze
Across the field, along the woods
Running fast…
Sliding off the saddle
Hanging on for my life
This makes me grip him more
He turns to me with a smile
"Now is the time to become as one!"

I see the fence grow near
Wide-open eyes gaze with fear
Fingertips tingle, muscles grow tense
Closer and closer, hooves of thunder
Listening to the horses pant, then silence…

Forever it felt to float above the fence
On that day, this I saw…

Clear the fence and earthbound law
There is a way, on my lips I prayed…

This fence we clear today!
With your help Lord, a strong horse we need!

Down to the ground we breeze...
As I turn behind, I see the fence still there
On the horse, father and son

For this day, we had no fear
Together again, one last fence to clear
Then off into the sunset, we disappear…

<u>night tears</u>

Sun's above the water, waves rolling by
-crest, hush, fade, goodbye, and disappear

Blue sky passes, diamonds shine high
-night lit with moon, brilliant beam I see

Touching sounds I hear
-moving feathers floating on air

On the ground for a moment
-back up to the sky

Thunder roars in my ear
-then fades with my fear

Down my face in a tear
-waves of diamonds

Caught with my hands
-they soon fall away

I see the moon cry
-when night becomes day

Sun's above the water, waves rolling by
-crest, hush, fade, goodbye, and disappear

Blue sky passes, diamonds shine high
-moving feathers floating on air

The wind brushes and caresses my face
-time never stands still in this place

Life I behold all around
-eruption shakes the ground

Peace, harmony, music I hear
-an embrace of love is near

Down my face a tear
-waves of diamonds

Caught with my hands
-they soon fall away

Forgiveness a gift for everyone
-a time and place will come

Cry like thunder, then melt away
-then night becomes day

ugly beast

Life hangs from this frame more loosely
-day by day

My reflection is not what I want to see
-in my mind

Change is unwelcome and predatory
-unrelenting and eventual

Age and time wear away the youth
-in my bone and muscle

Though I run, sometimes looking back
-I slip closer into the maw

Time, the ugly beast nips at my heels
-invisible, but always present

All crave more time, longer life
-mostly spent meaninglessly

Valued in our mind, some say priceless
-viewed as a whole, completeness

What has happened now, what will be...
-experience time, live the journey

Moments of brilliance come here and there
-gone never to return

In one sense, time is true... it never lies
-Dependable as a mirror's reflection

Perfect imperfection slowly ticks away
-unseen shadow in the light

Time has value in what is left behind
-sacrifice, kindness, love most of all

Wrapped in a package with a smiling face
-twinkle in the eye

Sensitive touch, the laughter, the tear
-reflections of strength and fear

In the end, it's the ugly beast *time* I love
-for the chance to live

Serving the maker of time until journey's end
-shadow, reflection, love that shines

on the skin

Pictures on skin these shapes begin
In someone's mind
Slowly they become part of a life
Morning to night, always in sight

Fingernails change and so does hair
Tattoos remain permanent walking art
On the road or while asleep
Penetration deep into the skin
Forever along for the journey
No matter how long or how far

Hidden under clothes or out in front
Everyone can see...
But the meaning not known...
Sadness, joy or just me…
I want to be free!

There's hate in some tattoos
Bright colors, too...
Can't understand why?
Ink your body and skin
Get stuck with a needle and pin

There must be lots of pain when done
And after a scar that sticks with you
A part of your body on display
This picture I made on my body today

Man or woman, a tattoo, body art
A new name, just me
Pictures without a wall
Everywhere, at work and at the mall
On airplanes, buses and trains
At the park and baseball games

I've seen friends get tattooed
I, too, wanted one
But now I think…why this desire?

To tell a story, remember past glory
One detail that gives me thought
Does the tattoo die too?

From dust, life, back in the ground
Perhaps like a face or a picture
People see who we once were

Walking *ART,* a piece of history
Never understood, just a mystery…

oak tree

Standing at the very top of the hill
Looking over the valley quiet and still
Everyone sees branches rising high

Thick solid trunk down into the ground
Cool, soft, blanket of shade all around
Resting place where birds fly and make nests
This place I like the best!

Climb up the side, out on a limb
From there watching all below
After some time, see a man under the tree
Holding a cloth in his hand

Into the tree he placed the cloth
There in a small nook hidden away
Where no one could see…

Soon he walked away and down I climbed
Curiosity and wonder tempting me, I looked!
For I just had to see what he placed in the tree

My hand felt a cloth, grasping it tight…
So not to drop or for it to get lost!
What was it and how much did it cost?
Then just when I was about to unfold the cloth…

A hand on my shoulder made me jump, then fall
Rolling over on my back that same man I saw…

His hand outstretched, wanting his goods
Out of my hand "and" into his pocket it went!
He turned away and began to walk

"Before you leave sir, may I ask?
What do you keep in the old, oak tree?
To no one I will tell, not a single soul…"

"If you promise to never come here again
I will show you young man"

Thought for a minute, and then said,
"Sir this is my oak tree too, I come when I will"

"My boy, you're right", he said and into my hand
Placed the cloth, then whispered in my ear…

Never have I gazed upon what was inside…
Quickly I placed it into the tree to hide!
But the whisper to you, I will confide…

"Guard your oak tree well
And your secrets never tell"

Over the hill he vanished, never to be seen again…

The secret kept, then forgotten as a dream
Occasionally check in the nook of the oak tree
Always the cloth, resting safely I would see-

After growing and moving away
Years later to that tree I returned…
At the top of the hill, in the waves of grass
Stood the old, oak tree…

Closer I walked, wondering what I would see…
To the branch where I used to sit...
Watching birds, dreaming of wonder, today I look!
So down I climbed, my hand into the nook

Holding the cloth, grasping it tight
Slowly uncovering the mystery of the land…
There I saw a stone, gleaming as a mirror
And my reflection which had grown old

One last look at the old, oak tree
Over the horizon to where the sun sets
Now is my time to walk over the hill and…

For me time will stand still
Now, forever and until…

Free…

<u>mist</u>
Deep in the land with old, tall trees…
In mountains far away, rests a ring of mist…
There… rays of sunlight rarely beam
Every sound can be heard

Water flowing in the stream
Down the mountainside
Eyeing a gracefully falling waterfall
A rise of mist, sunlight rays, fresh and new
Ever changing shadows of blue
On my face, it stays with my hands
Out of the maze, through the mist
Step by step, hill by hill

A stone picked upon the path
Then tossed into the mist
Tearing through the leaves
Finally coming to rest…
Another thrown, ricocheting…

Sounds of birds, animals echo
Animals far, some near
Endless trails, a vernal path unbeaten
One gets lost looking for clues…
Resting for a moment
Smell the forest and the lofty trees

Overhead in the distance, the waterfall
Resonance ringing, snared within the mist…
How did I come to be in this place?
Do I require liberty?
It appears safe, but hidden mystery I fear

Forbidden puzzle that haunts without refrain
Fables, tales, myths, legends and fantasy…
Some remarkable, thoughtful, and austere
Courageous and humorous…
It does not apply to the compass

Truths, images, touch and smell
A curious idea for my ear, the bell
After touching the mist, will I wake?
Can I return to the world I know?
Do I remain in this realm?
Ever searching for the mystery?

Continuing the venture...
My hand struggles to rouse the mist
First I recoil, hesitate, and doubt…
Then terror of not knowing what will occur…
Slowly my hand reaches out to the fog

Then both engage to be free...
Unshackle, arouse my flesh and blood

On the frontier near my destination
Everything alive, bonding, flowing…
Falling notes, musical flutes, down the falls

Along the mountainside fusing sunlight
Busting into the surface of the lake
Broad and bright, a heavenly sight…

My eyes open, time is brief
The signal I've heard…
In the early dawn and at midnight
Movement with action
Humming, then a song…
Crying, laughter, love that's strong
Hunger and desire, filling me with life

Being born a joyous sight for all
Especially for mother, father standing tall

Today I rest and sleep, then early at dawn
Live this gift of life before chance is gone...

machines

Obsolete quickly before year's end
Special-special, buy new, don't mend
Horsepower slower, Nobel prize winner
Capital lush silicon valley
Home-grown pioneers with talent
Ground-breaking technology
A wristwatch device
Implanted, let's roll the dice

Astounding they say...
Above accomplishment and beyond...
Steady stream, steady stream
Innovation-innovation-machines!
How about some coffee and cream?

Friction in culture
Don't know what people want?
Everything's expensive, detached
No value, just cost
New firms appear!
Rising up to the air!
Connected to everyone, everywhere!
For brother, sister, mother and dad

Here it is or on the way
All you have to do is pay
In all countries, a vending machine
How about some coffee and cream?

Special-special, entertainment for me
Tired in the morning after I wake
Tired in the afternoon, take a break
Tired at night, turn off the light
My language, my home, my life, my dream
How about some coffee and cream?

Night is silence for me...
Some space to be free...
To close my eyes, a hope and wish
Special-special, low cost too
Nothing else can compare, easy to clean
How about some coffee and cream?

Air, sunshine, wind, special as can be
Time spent with family and friends
Watching children grow
How much does this cost?
Special-special, priceless in fact!
Nothing like I've ever seen!
How about some coffee and cream?

brand new

There is a smell that's pleasing, a very special smell
  A man made smell of something new and fresh
Shine and glimmer, afraid to touch…
  Polish everyday, protection a must
Delicate, never lasting, soon turning to dust
  In the end, never worth very much
Kept for a while and precious to us
  To show to others and let them gently brush

Mighty mountains far away high
  Dream place or in my backyard
Changing, brand new everyday
  Lush green grass, an eclipse of yellow leaves
Tree trunks round, climbing to the sky so blue
  This is brand new, not man made
People question each other for an answer
  Day after year after century after here…
So beautiful it is to view…
  Not man made-then by whom?

Sunrise dawn, sunset dusk, sleep and dream
  Joy and sadness, cry and scream
It's all around but I can't see above beyond…
  Great rivers cut frozen, earth-ice, north-south
Awesome beauty abounding everywhere
  Can it be explained with mere words, by mouth?

One and all in pairs, two by two
 Birth, death this is true…
In between, what should I do?
 Rain in the afternoon, lakes-oceans
Not man made-then by whom?

A few are forced to submission by threat
 Some wait for the answer revealed
Others look deep to unlock the buried truth
 Some are deceived, just writing on the wall
Know the question and the call
 Who made life and who made me?
I want to explain with words from my mouth
 Man cannot make man nor his soul
Or change the sky from blue

 There is a truth and there is faith
It was given to us at an early date
 Long ago with just a breath…
Free will and choice follow, only one rule
 It could not be kept, broken by a fool
Not man made-then by whom?
 When does our bell toll?
All under God's control
 Everything forever, all brand new!

circles and squares

Bricks in the wall stopping me cold
  Use them as a tool, this I learned
Under my feet, everywhere I go
  Squares and more squares, up-down
All through the hall and through town
  Patterns of squares in many designs
Mosaics of history in a straight line
  Used to measured distance
How far do I go?

Imagine the squares from head to toe
  Flags on posts on rooftops too…
Squares of every color and every hue
  I sit on them to eat my food
Squares to please and change my mood
  Squares to live in, angles I choose
Squares in circles, under my shoes
  Square TVs, windows and doors

Some with shape or flat on the floor
  Waiting to be opened or protect
Squares are easy, connecting dots, lines
  A world is round as the sun that shines

Circles go places, squares slide in grooves
  Circles are free and always come around
Sometimes faster if not gravity bound
  Squares go clunk whenever they fall
Circles bounce up and roll along tall

Games are played with circles and spheres
  Golf, baseball, soccer, basketball, checkers
Circles and squares together forever…
  Lost coins sometimes on the ground
Ice cubes in a glass, that's round
  Squares melting to circles, new shape found

Four corners two, are not new
  Not a new invention, it's been around
Geometric designs in every room
  Even our mysterious moon
Instruments that play a tune

So married are the circles and squares
  Always forever, sometimes in pair
It's not the ocean that's flat
  But the universe that's square
And falling is dangerous, so take care
  In circles of unknown, courageous dare

millie's trip

Over and over she asked, "When can we go?
I'm ready! What are we waiting for? Lets go!"
So today is the day, pump up the tires
Oil the chain and check the breaks

Out the gate we went and up the hill fast
To the first intersection
No fear, a very brave little girl
Then down the hill holding the breaks
Careful and calm she rode, amazed I stood
She had learned well, improved her skill
This was real bike riding
Not in the yard or in the park...

Alert she was as we approached a steep hill
What a hill! How would she do?
A first-time experience, this was all new
We stopped to take a look
Her confidence and courage shone through
Soon she would go on bike rides alone
Down the hill, rolling fast at high speed
She held the bike straight and true
Enjoying every moment until the last
We parked our bikes all in a line

And then we went into a store
What we bought is a forgotten thought
Only the bike ride, I remember that day
After some time we were on our way

"What about the hill on the way home?
It is very steep! Do we walk?" she asked
"This time the hill we climb," I said

On the bike she stood
Pushing with all of her might and heart
Around the peddles went slowly
"Peddle hard, peddle hard
We'll make it to the top, push hard!"

Once there, we took a drink and felt the joy
This special moment, once in a lifetime
For the rest of the trip, I then knew
Millie's first step and now a bike ride too
The world, an adventure she'll go and seek
This first bike ride is our memory to keep
When we talk of that day
Pride and joy I feel
My little girl has grown fast and high
Special and precious days have passed
Before my eyes...

tunnel

Light outlines the opening
Shadows deep inside
Ever changing as I move
Closer to chamber wide
The sheen ebbs from
The subterranean chasm
Doubt and anxiety
A dash of sweat beads up
As I move closer
Closer to the entrance

Inside there is no light
Only glow of night
Pulsating reverberations
Seen on the wall
Emulating my movements
As I crawl

Shadows come from shadows
Bright and dim shapes
Characters, many kinds
Sounds magnify
The depth I've come
Drops of water echo

An endless tide
My breath is short
No end in sight
Passageways that grow...
Dim from no light
Groping for what I believe
There is to find

To undercover wonders
Seen in my mind...
A reason for being here
Waiting-waiting-waiting...
For something to happen...

Then a stream of light
Shining bright
Pierces the darkness!
Beckoning me to follow
So I must!
Suddenly thoughts of fear...
No end in sight...legs that float...
Reflection of light
In pools of water
My mantle, my starlight
Sensing cold damp air around me

Foul, pungent, a life of it's own
Fight to get clear, free to my goal
Escape but to where?
The path has not appeared
When or where will it be found?
On the stone wall, I pound and pound

Have I taken the long and hard way?
Always dark and always gray
Up above is where I should look
A place where it's bright and day
The focus is wide and to a point
Reaching forever, boundless...
Shed all, become a pioneer
Imagine no limitation, none at all

No horizon - time unknown
Tunnels I remember everywhere
Everything I've seen
Read, touched and heard
Put into a special place

One way in - one way out…
Connecting to each other
On and on…

Endless tunnels of life…
Lost for a time - new day by day…
Dark and unclear
Scant light holding fear

Every time the clocks tick away
A tear falls from my eye
Slowly moving to the edge
Over to an opening
Turning back many times
Getting lost...
Looking around the corners
Not knowing what I'll find
One time in - one time out
Time ticking away, tunnels winding…

Never stop looking back
Always look ahead
Sometimes wait-
Sprint to be free-
Life…hope…love…joy…trials…
The stories continue…
Turn the page…
Don't close the book
Grasp the key, unlock the cage!

sweet music

Whistle... a natural sound
Hum... a morning tune
Vibration... in the afternoon
Drum... when night comes

Befit my voice
Laughter, cries, beating heart
Made from a piece of wood
Or steel that glows

Spreading through and filling the room
Looking for an ear to feed
An echo floating on the wind
Then silence that grows

Hungry for more...
I catch a dancing note
Before it hits the floor

And there is no way
To set it free...
In the end...
It must die with me...

far east

Maps - show places
One - wants to travel
Go there - then back return
In a wink of an eye
Many things - are not said...

People - culture - language
Discover - study - learn
Food - clothing - life

Greeting - farewell
Bow - handshake - wave
Smile - a pat on the back

Festival - dance
Great big drums...
New life...
When the rising sun comes

Thinking of cherry blossoms
For their short life - people sing
Return - next year...
Good weather - happiness brings...

balloons

Air of life held for a time, floating free…
Quiet, peaceful, only the wind
A whistle and ring of a bell
Off in the distance, blue skies and time…

A baby, best friend, sometimes love
Sunrise and sunset, my pet
Hello hugs or waves goodbye
Birthday party, a picnic day
Precious things soon go away

Spring, summer, fall and winter
Catching fish, swimming in a river
Playing in piles of leaves
Making a snowman
Working hard, getting coins
Precious things soon go away

Climbing a tree, riding a bike
Flying down a slippery slide
Floating rivers, twinkling stars
Letting a balloon go free
Forever, precious memories stay

spontaneous

Change my mind...

You dare ask such a thing? Impossible!
Imagine all of the problems it might bring
Think of everything I would have to do…
Once I make up my mind, it's too late-
There's no way it can be done-
I'll fight the idea until I've won
Change is surprise and shock
Too sudden to comprehend…
Firm in my mind and never bend
Believe I'll have second thoughts?
Surmise that I'll give in to change?
Do you understand the difficulty
All this change could bring?
I'm sorry, I just have to say "No thank you"
Never going to revert, switch or rearrange
No more talk of this sudden shock
I'm a wall, an unbreakable rock
Nothing you can say or do…
You can't tell me anything new…
Well, just this once…
What do you want to change?

born in austria

Morning rises, night sets
Just like any other place

Flags blow in the wind
Tablecloths of lace

Old wood, tall mountains
Fresh air to breathe

Sweet music plays
Pastry tickles the tongue

Mine and Mozart's home
Many songs are sung

Stay for a time
Make new friends

A birthplace found
To someday return

On my face this is worn
Austria is where I was born

lights

Out of the night shine…
…brilliant objects…
…from far away and beyond-
Seen for a period of time…
…studied and written about…
…songs that are sung-
Attracted we are, by the glow…
…connected they are by…
…some odd equality all in a row-
Distance of light measured…
…with one's eye…
…watching them as they fly-
Falling slowly, floating…
…lightning flash of glare…
…sparkling in the air…
…silent speed to comprehend…
…grasp then share-
Perpetual celebration for humanity…
…explore…dream…pioneer…
…infinite, sometimes ignored…
…forgotten, then witnessed-
Oblique midnight sky…
…divine wonder, and angelic lights-

secret ants

Small builders, workers in another world
Seen from the outside, do they see us?
Is that why they run and hide?

Do ants have a secret
What don't they want anyone to know?
I wonder what it could be...
To investigate, we must go down low
Ants live deep under the earth's crust

Is there something about us?
What don't they trust?
Most people, especially kids
Just want to watch as they carry sand
Giggling and teasing the ants

One ant is not powerful, but many?
A different story, frightening, crawling
Under the floor, up the wall
Their secret we'll never know
Unknown for quite a while
So let's get along with them
Lend each other a smile

art

Secret of life for all revealed
Painted canvas through the years
Designs/buildings/bridges
Landscaped gardens of kings

Sport at its best/winners/losers
Shrill/suspense/thrill/expectation

Trains on tracks
People breaking their backs

Stories written/passed on
For generations to come

Anything the mind can conceive
All can see/some will believe

New ideas/very few indeed
Hope for a happy harvest
As we sow our seeds

Fresh style follows old trends
Invention is what I read

A Nobel Prize/a trophy to keep
Prize for art/sacrifice then weep

Signature or brand/famous name
Learn the rules/then play the game

The eye of the beholder
Fool with wisdom/unlimited space

Beautiful sight/horizon over the hill
Moon/white light/stars at night

Absolute/boundless wilderness
Mine to control

Borders welcome/this is our hope
Last chance/uncertainty

Wash away/welcome the storm
See it there right in front of you
See it there a part of you

Rainbow colors cover
Day and night
True love holds tight

belly flop

Splat...

Through the body...

Total pain burning...

Forest fire speed...

Waiting for it to stop...

Slowly disappear...

Memories to keep...

Locked away somewhere...

Instant fear, happiness cheer...

Falling...

Waiting to be caught...

for all

cry-smile-scream...

live-love-dream...

sit-stand-stare...

hope-wish-dare...

touch-taste-feel...

remember-think-speak...

youth-age-time...

see-witness-show...

care-help-share...

recollect-know-forget...

idea-imagine-create...

gift-grace-salvation...

the smart one

Which one are you?
Was the question asked?

Which one? Was the reply

Yes, which one are you?
Was asked again

Which one?
Is that what you asked?

Yes, yes, yes,
Again and again
Which one are you?

I'm afraid I don't understand

It's very simple, not hard to say
I must know before I let you...
Go on your way...

A riddle I must know before I pass?

Now you've got it
That's what I need

Can I have another clue?
Your question is unclear...

Sorry, no other clues
Only what I said
And again I say
Which one are you?

To that I can only say...
If you think time...
Will bend, stretch, or expand...
Hold your breath
As long as you can
To the last moment
Just one second more

Heartbeat as a drum
For some, life is done...
For others, just begun...
I choose to be the smart one

You may continue on your way...

numbers

Thinking, dreaming, wishing...
Catching the big one
Time never ending, filling space
Forever endless...
Off to an invisible place

Seen only by me
Sometimes not forgotten
The next morning-
Starting a new day-
Watching people stare

A single thought begun
Counting endless numbers
That never equal sum
Round and round they go
Number one starts the show

Painting by the numbers
The picture is known
Painting with my mind
A picture hidden behind...
Sketching a dream for tonight
Sketching a dream for tomorrow
Sketching a dream until...

Step by step...
Day by day...
Week by week...
Month by month...
Year by year…
Decade by decade...
Century by century...
Time gone away…

Counting numbers everyday-
Continuing where others have stopped!
Line by line… block by block…
Covering what has happened in the past

The picture I paint with my mind
Left for others to understand
My job done?
Not until the color is added
To my piece of the puzzle
Incomplete without one's life

With me, the end of a song
New life will grasp the truth
Share the picture behind your eyes...

water

Glass raised to one's lips;
Water trickles on the tongue!

Cold refreshing sensation;
Held by the hands!

Ice cubes rattle;
Up the glass tips!

Into the body flows;
From the foundation of life!

To cleanse and purify;
The great need!

Pure crystal clear liquid of life;
Quench my thirst!

Just the sight of it flowing;
Fills me with joy!

Let me be first;
To wish you cheer!

the shells

Washed up on the shore
In the middle, on the line
Surrounded by land
Under the brilliant sun
Noise all around
Floating by unbound
Waiting for the next wave
To come around

Destination, not my choice
Quiet whisper in my voice
Changing horizon night and day
No glimmer of how long I'll stay

Bright morning sun
Perhaps clouds of gray
Washed by pearls of raindrops
They show me the way

Seized by a rolling wave
Out far beyond we fade
Stability the goal of this affray
Mystery of where next we lay

Thrown up high with the wind
Pulled down under the wave
Endless cycle is where I'm pinned
Round and round I pave

Can that be land in the distance?
Coral blue water, white arena
On an explosive battlefield
Power surges, destiny sealed

Helpless in the ventilating mist
With nothing or no one to cling
An anchor of iron is what I sing
Always a fingertip from my fist

Closer the land becomes
Hope grows strong with desire
Give this fragile life more time
Presence narrow and localized

The direction known, off I tread
My right allowed and fought for
Makers of freedom for all
Spoken for all to hear

Missed opportunity gone always
Strength did not conquer my fear

day dreaming

Looking through the windshield
Scorching sun burning the ground
Stones on fire glowing red hot!

Silence like I've have never heard…
A smell in the air that's burned

Wind rolls over the ground
Carving dust and my soul

Seems a hopeless place
To be stuck

A broken down Plymouth
Steam rising from under the hood

Time blowing away
With the dirt and dust

It's been a while now...
Every direction I look...
Desert, rocks, and silence…

Some water and my guitar*
The road ahead…

Down the ribbon of road I go
A glance back to see the dead metal

Making tracks under the sun
Hoping for a ride to come

Here, I see it coming…
Over the hill

Z-28 downshifting fast, low gear growl
Ride, soldier on leave, going home?

Loud radio, Lynard Skynard
That smell that surrounds you
The driver buries the pedal…
We blaze over hills

To a train station, drop me off
So long and farewell, my ticket bought

An old train station
Oak benches and floor
Colorado Rocky Mountains

Whistle train roar
Board my train
On my way home

Lots of time to daydream
Traveling all alone

Just my guitar and camera
A photo of the railroad station

Through the mountains long
A river, a railroad crossing

Daydream home
This endless trip
Through the mountains
Ride the whip

Roller coaster
One life headed home

Up and down
We roam...

Never the same
After a long daydream...

hide and seek

Leaning against a tree with my hands
Over my eyes
Counting to one hundred

At that moment everyone scatters
Disappearing into the night
While I count, I hear voices
Whispers, cracking branches and twigs

A dog barks, I open my eyes
To the sight of the bark on the tree
Suddenly I'm mesmerized
By the shape and texture

Then I realize!
It is alive…

Stationary, having been that way
For quite some time
Massive, big as a house

For a moment, I try to wrap my arms
Around the trunk...

Impossible for me to even
Think of such a thing

My gaze falls downward to the roots
Huge legs that penetrate deep
How far into the ground
So incredible, no one can say

I notice carved into the tree
Some names unknown to me

Thinking why not...
Do the same!

I take my pocketknife out
And start carving my name
Into the timber

Now, so long after...
Is the tree still there?
Do kids play games?
Climb up the branches?

Traveled back to that place I did
An open space is all that's left
Hide and seek, lost fancy of the past

tri-tone

Three sounds in one
Which one will come?
All fit the key, up or down
Timeless universe
Bottomless pit of sound

Reflecting mirror of what is heard
Suddenly an added word
Harmonics, intricate detail unknown
Incomprehensible, only guess
Perhaps luck

Melody, step by step
Some skip two steps, some skip three
Repetition that sounds different
Together or alone
Tri-tone... give me a song

Show me a rhythm to count
Display what belongs
Puzzle of sound
Some pieces found
How do I know what is next?

How do I wake the music?
The notes that sleep
This mountain steep
This ocean deep

Put music on my fingertip
Out of nowhere please
Tri-tone golden sound
Merry-go-round

Playful, endless and forever
Exciting to the ultimate degree
Breathtaking, a lump in my throat

Trapped in my mind
Waiting to be found
I'm still here earthbound
Every noise and sound
Wearing a mask
Hiding blind

In our soul it rests
Until needed
Born protected and fed
Home in a nest
Longing to be lead

picture sky blue

Bigger then men they stand
Corporate hands
Leading me to their land

What is a black hole?
How can it suck all of life
Into the size of a pin?

There is no understanding
This does not comprehend

A program fed to people
Without having a choice
Living without a voice

The grip is held
Who are they?
Babbling about
Eating my life

I am not a meal
Not for sale
Not food for thought

Search for how to live
An idea sought
Purpose, most of all
Desire to climb
Move mountains

Here and now are clear
Yesterday is over...
Today is happening...
Tomorrow will change...

Mystery and fear surround
Countless notions
Enter and exit
Influenced from life

Born pure, always growing
Difficult to stay that way
Slowly learning...

Perform what one thinks is true
Do what one imagines is new
Perception a vista, a splendid view

Priceless and not just for a few
Picture sky blue...

mars

Have we hit the jackpot?
Astronomers are profound
News, places, craters abound
Wonderland of rocks to examine
Evidence of water, close-up view

Spacecraft orbit, I only see the moon
Mapping and naming places
More missions to come

Birth of comets
Exploration, gravitation, storms
A rogue meteorite

People are stunned, have no idea
Cosmic dust, year after year
Red planet so far, just a dot
In the night sky

What has been told and written
Must be true
History's song sung by everyone
Living here, there, everywhere...

Black and white scroll
Carved in stone
On statues and on walls
Buried deep, covered with red dust

Mars surrounded by stars
Rovers relay information
Signals coming in
Speaking to us now

Science fiction to us
Story of space
Is this a wisp of air?

I'm not on Mars
Not on the moon
What is the truth?
Perhaps we'll know soon

What about the other planets
Can we explore them too?

How long will all of this take
I'm ready to celebrate
Count down commence
10 9 8 7 6 5 4 3 2 1 - run... run... run...

it's a town

Two miles away, easy to find
A saw mill on the left
Logs piled everywhere up high
Sawdust blowing across the street

At the first intersection
A root beer stand
Classic hamburger with fries, a coke

Corner store with a crooked floor
Golf course, country club
Weddings, parties, fun, fun, fun

Two-story homes paginate the road
Into the small town, suddenly a hill
Coasting down and around
More houses, Carnegie library
Public high school

National Guard Armory
Vogue theater, Ben Franklin
Coast to Coast store
Taverns and bars...

I can't remember all the names
Can't even count the number
As many as the stars

Catholic elementary
Fence around the playground
Limestone bank, two huge columns
They reach to the roof

Railroad tracks, two sets in fact
Police station on the corner
Small fire truck

Chicken factory, farmers near
Summer celebration
Parade held downtown

Star on top of a hill at the edge of town
Glowing brightly, evening until dawn

Football, baseball, swimming
The city dump next door
Shooting rats at the city park

Piles of garbage mixed together
A foul smell indeed

Bowling alley, elegant restaurant
River, two bridges, spring overflow

Only two thousand people
And still the same today

Some things new
No theater or Coast to Coast
Ben Franklin too is gone

It's a small town
Like many others
Holding memories
Good and bad

No special place
Just where I lived
Where I come from

Visit once in a while
See some old friends
Talking about the old days
Always brings a smile

Counted time gone by
In the vault of my mind

lines

Thin, thick, bold, broken, hollow
 -still a line-
Straight or curved, angled fine
 -still a line-
One after another
 -still a line-
Vertical, horizontal, behind
 -still a line-
In my hand to measure
 -still a line-
Erase or sign
 -still a line-
Patterns, shapes from the sky
 -still a line-
Rays of sunshine
 -still a line
Fingerprints, one of a kind
 -still a line-
My legs, footprints
 -still a line-
Long, straight highway
 -still a line-
Trees standing tall
 -still a line-

No trespassing sign
 -still a line-
Borders of countries
 -still a line-
Rivers flowing fast
 -still a line-
Fishing poles and pencils
 -still a line-
Braille for the blind
 -still a line-
Libraries stacked with books
 -still a line-
Lightning from the sky
 -still a line-
Vineyards for wine
 -still a line-
Circles, X's, tic-tac-toe
 -still a line-
Flags blowing in the wind
 -still a line-
Sound barrier, broken time
 -still a line-
Arms, legs, hair, finger pointed
 -still a line-
Claiming your property
 -That line is mine-

the beginning

What is that?
Where did it come from?
Why did it happen?
Who did it?
When will it end?

Questions abound?
Silence...
Answers...
No sound...

Waves of white water
Soaring to reach the sky
Touching clouds to be one
Bubbling between my toes

A feather falls to the ground
Slowly gliding back and forth
Up, then down
Sudden shift on the wind

Gusts taking it higher
Above all the trees

Watch with wonder
Then gone from sight

As one turns day to night
Remember yesterday?
How much fun
Can't wait until tomorrow comes

Candles flicker in the window
Melting slowly, overflowing
Giving away all of their light
Keeping the shadows bright

Outlining the wall
Lines into shapes
Soft, glowing amber
My hands on fire

Moving, flames leaping
My hands abrade
Over my face

The warmth paints
Abruptly gone
Replaced by cool, fresh
Moist, clean air

What is that?
Where did it come from?
Why did it happen?
Who did it?
When will it end?

Questions abound…
Silence…
Answers…
No sound…

From outside, it flows to my ear
Music natural, closer and closer
Then very near
Into my soul transfixed

With the window open
A breeze rolling through
A feather floats into my room
Up then down, back and forth
Resting in my clasped hands

As I open them, life I see
All there, lee of me
Whistling a song, a simple melody
Asking to be set free

Flutter away all grown up
Time to make your own way
Flame outside sweeps to my heart
A voice never heard
Come in, open the door
Now this place forevermore

What is that?
Where did it come from?
Why did it happen?
Who did it?
When will it end?

Questions abound…
Silence…
Answers…
No sound…

Rules learned, followed, query
Experience to gain, to survive
Up the sun, sleep the dawn
King, Queen, pawn
Play the game
Use your gift of life
Bloom beautiful, graceful, brilliant
Be alive…

natural

Rocks, grass, earth…
    -roots down deep
Sweat, water, ice…
    -rain on my face-
Birds, butterflies, rabbits…
    -path in the trees-
Sky, clouds, stars…
    -dream in my mind-
Thunder, lightening, fire…
    -wild-burning energy-
Tears, joy, laughter…
    -emotions from the heart-
Running, jumping, falling…
    -actions experienced everyday-
Handshake, hug, kiss…
    -hello, I miss you-
Walking, eating, sleeping…
    -becomes a daily routine-
Party, dance, life…
    -the best time I've ever had-
Time, forever, eternity…
    -a day in the sun-

the nose

Silently moving behind the scene
Information unknown, ears cold
Without caution, other side not told

Using the past as a hammer
Crushing all spirit that remains
Arguments paint shame

Now age begins to show
The future grows short
No feeling, mocking still

Alone, spat out with the bone
Buried deep in the ground
Waiting to be found

I don't understand
Why it's taking so long
Soon the waiting will end

Change and bend
Time does the same
I've forgotten my name…

all alone

One sober afternoon
Snow falling gently, quietly

I'm cold…
But the enjoyment of the day
Lets me dream…

The grassy surface covered
As I watch the graceful snowflakes
Glide down into a blanket

No windows in this old shed
Once a house to man's best friend
Max and Buster
Now since gone

Only me…
Staring out…
Through a door that doesn't close
Frozen in the ground…

Through the cracks of the wall
Light splits and blazes

Reflecting spangle of tinsel
Spider webs radiate and glow
Hanging from the ceiling corner

I see…
A worn out floor
That has now
Become part of the earth

Out the door I look again
Cushions of diamonds
As far as I can see
Still floating everywhere

No one in sight
More snow falling
Faster and faster still

Solemn echoes in my mind
Beating like a drum
Pounding snow

My imagination paints images
One last look through the door
Snow dangling from my eyes
My footprints are covered…

last time he cried

One small boy walking
Across the school yard
As on every weekday, lunch was ready
Nearby he lived and home he went
Only more people present this day
Some of them unknown
Vacuous faces that quietly stare
This is strange he thought to himself...
Are we having a party?
What event are we celebrating today?
On the weekend, many he has seen…
But never during the week
Food on the kitchen table
Plates and cups piled high

What a strange party again he thought
All were sad and some with tears
Again and again they began to cry
Still the boy wondered at the sight
Suddenly it hit the boy, a terrible loss
This is what it must be…
Over near the window his sisters sat

Where they once had laughed…
And jumped for joy…
Over on the sill with red faces
Sadness falling from their eyes
One older and the other younger
Sunlight pouring into white curtains
Painting the wood in amber light

Mother on the sofa tearful
Looking helpless and surprised
Whispers become echoes
Then thunder in the boy's ear

Now he knew why everyone was there
All of his energy fell down to the floor
Down to his knees, catching tears…
Wiping them onto his clothes
Biting his numb hand

Never again...
Sit on his father's knee…
Hear his father's laugh…
Hear his father's roar…
Wait for him to come home…
Wipe the tears and again never cry...
Never again…Look into his father's eye...

time lapse

What did I just do?
Where did I put my…?
Who was I going to call?
How will I survive?
When did I meet you?

Every morning, endless routine…
Waking up from a dream
Short memory forgotten
Why do I dream?
What do they mean?

Another place, my mind floats…
Traveling for pleasure
This is a nightly trip
Escape for a while
Then return to life

Terror, guilt placed on the weak
Powerless to battle back
Then into the wind I stand
With my arms I rear and slice
Waking up from life…

all together highway

Bridled, joined, made that way
Side by side, empty, flat and round
Two or more directions, back and forth
Many directions, destinations, ports

Flowing into each other, highways run
Following them, boring, interesting, fun
A road for everyone...

Length, width, challenge, here it comes
Pounding the pavement, sounding a drum
Last drowning prayer for hope, salvation

Silver spoon, success, winning, a champion
Treadmill of life, cog in the wheel
Turning endlessly until one disappears
Behind, in front, I see the same
Others, many playing the routine game

Footsteps on wheels, flying in the air
Train, boat, new clothes to wear
Waiting everyday, slipping and sliding
On the all together highway

done

What do I do now?

One good idea I need
A list I'll make
Choose some deeds

That done...

Spell everything out
Plant the best seeds
Then watch my ideas grow

That done...

Ideas planted
Nurtured a bit everyday

Buried deep, growing straight
Slanted, tall, some not at all
Progress, a slow crawl

That done...
How do I choose?

Only by sight or height
Most people would
Select one that looks good

I've decided
I'm going to let the idea pick me
But when will I know
Or how will I be chosen

To every idea, I'll give a number
Then choose from a hat
With my hand I grasp

That done...

Now in my hand I hold
A single piece of thin paper
Delicate concept, a purpose
Perhaps perfection untold

This notion written
Will change my life
And everyone I know
Just to unfold and be done

It's number one!

chemical

Sweet this mixture, taste, smell
What is it, I can't tell

Carried by people, passed through the air
Floating along wildly without a care

Then it hits, a knockout punch
Floored for the count
Dazed a bit, but wanting more

Invisible and not for sale...

How is it acquired?
Who makes it?
Is it different for everyone?

Special formulas that match
Each individual person perfectly

Puzzles with pieces
That can't be seen...

Am I carrying a chemical?

Is someone waiting for it now?
I wonder who they are?
How will I know?
When it's passed on

This craving never disappears
It lingers continuously
Keeping one aware and alert

When this euphoric time
Transpires...
I enter a circumvolution
Spiraling into an unfurled run

The answer to this cryptic mystery
Veiled to all...
Until contact with an equal
To harmonize...

Then just as it splashes upon one
A falling, floating bubble
Vanishes into clear unseen space
Along with the radiant chemical

Trying to hold with a mighty grip
Frees itself to find another lodestone breath

hard look

Blinking steadily, fixed in one position
Watching all who pass by
Quickly, slowly, motionless...

Some smile to show happiness
Joy, sad or blue...
A few with nothing to do...

Nowhere to go, just in the picture
Taking up space for that moment
Some waiting alone, a few in line

Limited view, a straight line
Ahead, left, right, up and down
Wind, snow, cold and heat
Strangers and good friends
A place to meet

This ever present hard eye looks...
Registering life, saving moments
Flashes for the show, people confess
Mortals watched from the gallery
Soon the spectators evanesce...

up

Always looking in some direction
Side to side, behind or in front, up or down
If strange eyes meet, a safe place they spear
The floor... down
Picture... to the side
An echo... from behind
But... usually never up

People look up to see the sky...
Or a bird flying by...
When someone tries to interrupt...
An angry time...
A mountain steep to climb...
Clocks on the wall...
Schedules for trains and planes...
People that are tall...
Low doorways...
On one's back, slip and fall...

The only other time that I know...
When people pray for help and forgiveness...
That is a time, when up is a safe place...
Where there are no strange eyes...

dive

Tearing the wind-
Clutching the wind-
Conquering the wind-

Mysterious, staunch, untimely, dubious
Dissolving into space…
Disappearing without trace…
Quiet and peaceful

Then up with the wave
Throwing me in every divergence
Steeling my spirit…
Fashioning me to an obedient servant

Terror, out face, icy cold blood
Cringing until my muscles extend
Beyond ultimate resolution
Transform into an explosive force

My assemblage propels a scream
Parish to oblivion, buried to decay
Snap out from a chimerical dream
Existence…an abrupt breath of day

framed

Hanging around waiting for attention
Functionality my only purpose
Hoping to be part of the attraction

Decorated, carved, polished, trimmed
Silver and gold, beautiful…
Wood of depth and grain

Shape of geometric design
Glowing under a tungsten light flame
Warm all around, eye-level height

Passing heartbeats pound
Beauty on display
Famous painting in the frame

Unknown outside, all alone
Windows on walls
Taken from place to place

Worlds real and false, invisible…
Seen only by a painter's eye
Telling a story, asking why…

the container

Made durable
  Long lasting
Yet delicate
  Occasionally
Thrown away
  Without thought
Then chosen
  By another
Still useful
  One of a kind
Taken home
  For a smile
Soon passed on
  Still some hope
A place to rest
  Then age
Begins to show
  Repair is temporary
Repose short-lived
  Liberation thrills
Endurance ebbs
  Mindful neglect
Genius! An Eternal Favor…

left lost

Carried with me almost all of the time
Just this once forgotten

Frantic search for my words
Over my face a mask of concern

Precious notebook filled with ideas
Months of thoughts written down

They came to me at different moments
In a split-second gone, never to return

Never out of my sight...
This accumulation of words

In my bag, safe and sound
Now perhaps lost...never found

Secret treasure, buried deep...
My mind and body ache for the loss

Wondering where can it be?
As I sleep now, turning, tossing

Will it be found someday?
My thanks and a reward

Searching endlessly until I fall
Up and down a long dark hall

From the beginning, every word
Start again, my mind dancing

A song for lost words and stories
Life, time, world of rhyme

A piece of moonlight
Bright star shine

Glow on my soul
Warm me forever

Here I stand
With open arms

Please this one request
Before my eyes

Embracing love all around
Words my treasure found

The End

Graphics and cover

JBS

Books by John Siwicki

Poetry

Inflexation
Fences
The Poetry of Food and Drink
Warbles
Are You Casablanca

Novels

ExPRESSION

AWAKE ASLEEP DREAMING DEAD

DREAM KILLER

www.jsiwicki.com

infojsiwicki@gmail.com

www.ingramcontent.com/pod-product-compliance
Lightning Source LLC
Chambersburg PA
CBHW061740020426
42331CB00006B/1307